TO:

FROM:

Never lose hope. Storms make people stronger and never last forever.

Roy T. Bennett

I don't just wish you rain,
Beloved — I wish you the
beauty of storms

John Geddes

you can be in the storm, but
don't let the storm get in you

Joel Osteen

There are some things you learn best in calm, and some in storm

Willa Cather

Even in the midst of the storm the sun is still shining

Dayna Lovely

you can look at my palm and
see the storm coming. Read
the book of my life and see
I've overcome it.

Mary J. Blige

Even paradise sees its share of storms, but in the end, it's still paradise

Trevor Driggers

If you are strong enough,
you can enjoy even in the
middle of a storm!

Mehmet Murat ildan

No matter what storm you face, you need to know God loves you. He has not abandoned you.

Franklin Graham

Big storms create big captains and they destroy the little ones!

Mehmet Murat ildan

When you come out of the storm, you won't be the same person who walked in. That's what this storm's all about.

Haruki Murakami

You cannot forever escape from the storm; you must learn to stand up to it

Mehmet Murat ildan

you can't have the rainbow without the storm.

Shannon L. Alder

Joy weathers any storm:
Happiness rides the waves

Todd Stocker

FIFTH AVENUE
BUILDING

My peace I leave with you –
we saw how there is peace even
in the storm

Vincent Van Gogh

There are storms in your own life;
storms from a cleansed conscience
emerges a changed life

Billy Graham

Life isn't about waiting for the storm to pass...It's about learning to dance in the rain.

Vivian Greene

The storm came. Lives were washed away. Ancient pains resurfaced. Now it is time for a sea of change

Tavis Smiley

Storms make trees take
deeper roots

Dolly Parton